I0139913

The Radiance Of The Little Boy:

Embracing Self-Worth

By Aaron Fields

Illustrated By Umar Altaf

Copyright © 2024 Aaron Fields. All rights reserved.

Published by The Write Perspective, LLC

Dallas, Texas,

All rights reserved. No part of this book shall be reproduced or transmitted in any form or by any means, electronic, mechanical, magnetic, photographic including photocopying, recording or by any information storage and retrieval system, without prior written permission of the publisher. No copyright liability is assumed with respect to the use of the information contained in this book. Even though every precaution has taken in preparation of this book, the publisher/author assumes no responsibility for errors or omissions. Neither is any liability assumed for any damage that results from the use of the information in this book.

ISBN:978-1-953962-44-7

The happiness, beauty and good health that you see in a little boy's face is a blessing.

Aaron Fields

In a world that often fails to see,

The worth and beauty of the little boy's glee.

It's crucial for him to know and believe,

In his own strength, resilience and dignity.

With every step he takes, he will stand tall,

Embracing his heritage, standing proud and all.

For his worth is not defined by others view,

But by the love and respect he holds true.

In a society that may try to dim his light,

He will shine bright, with all his might.

For he is a beacon of hope and grace,

A symbol of strength in every space.

So let the little boy value himself,

For in his heart lies endless wealth

A treasure trove of wisdom and power,

A reminder that he is worthy every hour.

May he always remember that without a doubt,

His worth is infinite, inside and out.

For the little boy's value is beyond measure,

A testament to his beauty and treasure.

END

.

www.ingramcontent.com/pod-product-compliance
Lightning Source LLC
Chambersburg PA
CBHW040035110426
42741CB00030B/26